W9-AFV-426

SUPER CUTE!

Baby Sloths

by Kari Schuetz

BELLWETHER MEDIA • MINNEAPOLIS, MN

Note to Librarians, Teachers, and Parents:

Blastoff! Readers are carefully developed by literacy experts and combine standards-based content with developmentally appropriate text.

Level 1 provides the most support through repetition of high-frequency words, light text, predictable sentence patterns, and strong visual support.

Level 2 offers early readers a bit more challenge through varied simple sentences, increased text load, and less repetition of high-frequency words.

Level 3 advances early-fluent readers toward fluency through increased text and concept load, less reliance on visuals, longer sentences, and more literary language.

Level 4 builds reading stamina by providing more text per page, increased use of punctuation, greater variation in sentence patterns, and increasingly challenging vocabulary.

Level 5 encourages children to move from "learning to read" to "reading to learn" by providing even more text, varied writing styles, and less familiar topics.

Whichever book is right for your reader, Blastoff! Readers are the perfect books to build confidence and encourage a love of reading that will last a lifetime!

This edition first published in 2014 by Bellwether Media, Inc.

No part of this publication may be reproduced in whole or in part without written permission of the publisher. For information regarding permission, write to Bellwether Media, Inc., Attention: Permissions Department, 5357 Penn Avenue South, Minneapolis, MN 55419.

Library of Congress Cataloging-in-Publication Data

Schuetz, Kari.
 Baby sloths / by Kari Schuetz.
   p. cm. – (Blastoff! readers. Super cute!)
 Audience: K to grade 3.
 Summary: "Developed by literacy experts for students in kindergarten through grade three, this book introduces baby sloths to young readers through leveled text and related photos"– Provided by publisher.
 Includes bibliographical references and index.
 ISBN 978-1-60014-933-7 (hardcover : alk. paper)
 1. Sloths–Infancy–Juvenile literature. I. Title.
QL737.E2S375 2014
599.3'13–dc23
                                                                                      2013008244

Table of Contents

Sloth Pup!	4
Mom and Meals	6
Tree Time	12
Glossary	22
To Learn More	23
Index	24

Sloth Pup!

A baby sloth is called a sloth pup. It lives in **tropical** forests.

Mom and Meals

A sloth pup **clings** to its mom's fur.

It sleeps on
her chest while
she hangs
from a tree.

The young pup drinks mom's milk. Later it eats leaves and flowers.

Tree Time

A sloth pup stays high up in a tree. There it is safe from **predators**.

Its brown hair blends in with trees. Green **algae** on its hair helps it hide, too.

algae

The sloth pup hangs upside down. Its sharp **claws** wrap around branches.

claws

The sloth
pup eats and
sleeps while
it hangs.

It climbs down to go to the bathroom. It hugs the tree and does a potty dance!

Glossary

algae—green plant-like material

claws—sharp, curved nails at the end of an animal's fingers and toes

clings—hangs on tight and close

predators—animals that hunt other animals for food

tropical—found in places with warm weather

To Learn More

AT THE LIBRARY

Bleiman, Andrew, and Chris Eastland. *ABC ZooBorns!* New York, N.Y.: Beach Lane Books, 2012.

Cooke, Lucy. *A Little Book of Sloth.* New York, N.Y.: Margaret K. McElderry Books, 2013.

Lynette, Rachel. *Three-Toed Sloths.* New York, N.Y.: Bearport Publishing, 2013.

ON THE WEB

Learning more about sloths is as easy as 1, 2, 3.

1. Go to www.factsurfer.com.

2. Enter "sloths" into the search box.

3. Click the "Surf" button and you will see a list of related Web sites.

With factsurfer.com, finding more information is just a click away.

Index

algae, 14
bathroom, 20
blends, 14
branches, 16
chest, 8
claws, 16, 17
climbs, 20
clings, 6
dance, 20
drinks, 10
eats, 10, 18
flowers, 10
fur, 6
hair, 14
hangs, 8, 16, 18

hide, 14
hugs, 20
leaves, 10
milk, 10
mom, 6, 10
predators, 12
safe, 12
sleeps, 8, 18
tree, 8, 12, 14, 20
tropical forests, 4
wrap, 16

The images in this book are reproduced through the courtesy of: Eric Isselee, front cover, p. 17 (small); Mark Kostich, pp. 4-5; Age Fotostock/ SuperStock, pp. 6-7; Minden Pictures/ SuperStock, pp. 8-9; Vilainecrevette, pp. 10-11; Worldswildlifewonders, pp. 12-13; Hofmeester, pp. 14-15; Kjersti Joergensen, p. 14 (small); Wildlife Bildagentur GmbH/ Kimball Stock, pp. 16-17; Maxcam, pp. 18-19; Rodrigo Arangua/ AFP/ Getty Images/ Newscom, pp. 20-21.